## Scientists at Work

# Meteorologists

Heather Hammonds

Smart Apple Media

This edition first published in 2005 in the United States of America by Smart Apple Media.

Smart Apple Media
1980 Lookout Drive
North Mankato
Minnesota 56003

Library of Congress Cataloging-in-Publication Data

Hammonds, Heather.
  Meteorologists / by Heather Hammonds.
  p. cm. — (Scientists at work)
  Includes bibliographical references and index.
  ISBN 1-58340-542-9 (alk. paper)
  1. Meteorology—Vocational guidance—Juvenile literature. 2. Meteorologists—Juvenile literature.
  [1. Meteorologists. 2. Meteorology—Vocational guidance. 3. Vocational guidance.] I. Title.
  II. Scientists at work (Smart Apple Media)

  QC869.5.H36 2004
  551.5'092—dc22                                                    2003070416

First Edition
9 8 7 6 5 4 3 2 1

First published in 2004 by
MACMILLAN EDUCATION AUSTRALIA PTY LTD
627 Chapel Street, South Yarra, Australia, 3141

Associated companies and representatives throughout the world.

Edited by Sally Woollett
Text and cover design by The Modern Art Production Group
Page layout by Raul Diche
Illustrations by Alan Laver, Shelly Communications Pty Ltd
Photo research by Jesmondene Senbergs
Printed in China

**Acknowledgements**
The author and the publisher are grateful to the following for permission to reproduce copyright material:

Cover photograph: Meteorology students, courtesy of Mike Rosel, Bureau of Meteorology.

Bureau of Meteorology, pp. 12, 14 (top right), 15 (top right), 18 (left), 19 (all); Donna Dubberke, p. 22; Ian Forrest/Bureau of Meteorology, pp. 8 (all), 14 (top left, bottom left); David Johns/Bureau of Meteorology, p. 14 (bottom right); Mike Rosel/Bureau of Meteorology, pp. 5, 13; Corbis, p. 20; Digital Vision, p. 18 (right); Getty Images, p. 23; Image Library, p. 15 (middle right); Dennis Sarson/Lochman Transparencies, p. 15 (top left); Mary Evans Picture Library, p. 6; NASA, p. 9 (bottom); National Oceanic and Atmospheric Administration/Department of Commerce, pp. 9 (top), 19 (top and bottom right), 24, 25, 27; NOAA Photo Library, pp. 7, 11, 15 (middle left, bottom left), 16, 21; Photodisc, pp. 15 (bottom right), 17; Photolibrary.com/Agefoto, p. 30; British Antarctic Survey/Science Photo Library, p. 4.

**Author acknowledgements**
Many thanks to Donna Dubberke of the United States National Weather Service, for kindly agreeing to be interviewed for this book.

While every care has been taken to trace and acknowledge copyright, the publisher tenders their apologies for any accidental infringement where copyright has proved untraceable. Where the attempt has been unsuccessful, the publisher welcomes information that would redress the situation.

**Please note**
At the time of printing, the Internet addresses appearing in this book were correct. Owing to the dynamic nature of the Internet, however, we cannot guarantee that all these addresses will remain correct.

# Contents

**Glossary words**

When you see a word printed in **bold**, you can look up its meaning in the glossary on page 31.

# What is a meteorologist?

A meteorologist is a scientist who studies the Earth's weather, **climate**, and **atmosphere**.

Some meteorologists study the day-to-day weather. They provide daily weather forecasts for the public and create weather maps, such as the ones we read in newspapers or see on television. Other meteorologists study long-term weather patterns and try to predict what the weather will be like in the weeks and months ahead.

Meteorologists may specialize in studying certain types of weather, such as tropical weather, polar weather, **hurricanes**, and storms. They may work at sea, or in remote places like Antarctica. They may even chase **tornadoes**!

Meteorologists use many different scientific instruments to gather information about the weather, climate, and atmosphere, to make weather forecasts. They measure weather conditions such as wind speed, rainfall, and temperature.

## Scientists working together

Meteorologists often work with other scientists, such as climatologists. Climatologists study the Earth's weather, climate, and atmosphere over long periods of time, to learn about long-term weather patterns, the environment, and climate change. Meteorology and climatology are **atmospheric sciences**.

**This meteorologist is using a weather balloon to study the weather.**

# The role of meteorologists

Meteorologists play a very important role in the community. Weather forecasting is an essential public service, and millions of people around the world rely on weather forecasts every day.

Public weather forecasts help us to decide what we will wear when we go out and what we will do during the day. They also allow us to plan our daily activities several days ahead.

Ships at sea and aircraft need special weather forecasts. The crew of ships and aircraft must know if high winds or stormy weather are expected. Forecasts help them to avoid these weather conditions and transport passengers and goods safely from place to place.

Farmers also depend on weather forecasts. They use daily forecasts and long-term weather forecasts to decide the best time to plant or harvest their crops, or to protect their livestock from bad weather. Long-term forecasts are very important to farmers and the community because they help farm production, ensuring a good supply of food and other farm products such as wool.

When extreme weather conditions such as thunderstorms, floods, hurricanes, or tornadoes are approaching, weather forecasts from meteorologists can save lives. People can take action to protect themselves and others if they know that bad weather is approaching. When wildfires threaten people and property, forecasts can show firefighters if the weather will be windy, hot, or cold, so they can plan the best way to fight the fires.

When extreme weather conditions are approaching, weather forecasts from meteorologists can save lives.

# Meteorology in the past

For thousands of years, people knew very little about the weather. Weather forecasting was based on **superstition** and **folklore**.

## Myths and sayings

In ancient times, the weather was often thought to be caused by gods or spirits. In ancient **Norse mythology**, Thor was the god of thunder. People thought the sound of thunder was made by the wheels of his chariot rolling along.

## Studying the weather

Some of the earliest people to study the weather scientifically were ancient Greeks. Greek scientists tried to explain what caused clouds, thunder, rain, hail, snow, wind, and other weather conditions. However, most of their explanations were wrong, because they had no scientific instruments to help them study the weather.

**Thor, Norse god of thunder**

## Key events in meteorology

**1500 B.C.**
During the Shang Dynasty, the Chinese keep the first regular weather records.

**340 B.C.**
Aristotle writes his book series *Meteorologica*.

**1593**
The thermometer is invented.

**1643**
The barometer is invented.

**1752**
Benjamin Franklin proves lightning is electricity.

**1803**
Luke Howard names cloud types.

**Early 1900s**
Sir Gilbert Walker makes connections with weather conditions in different countries on each side of the Pacific Ocean.

6

# Progress in meteorology

Scientific study of the weather advanced very little from ancient Greek times until the late 1500s and early 1600s.

## Keeping records

Important weather instruments such as the thermometer and the barometer were invented during the late 1500s and early 1600s. Scientists used thermometers and barometers to record changes in temperature and **air pressure** during different types of weather. Soon, meteorologists in Europe began to keep regular weather records.

During the 1700s and 1800s, much was learned about the weather. Weather instruments were constantly improving and weather stations were set up in many countries, to record the weather. In the late 1800s, meteorologists began to broadcast weather forecasts over long distances faster than ever before, using the **telegraph**.

## New instruments

During the 1900s came the greatest advances in meteorology yet. Modern instruments such as **radar**, satellites, and computers were invented. For the first time, meteorologists were able to track storms as they crossed the land, see weather conditions from space, and use computers to quickly process information about the weather.

Today, modern meteorologists are able to provide the most accurate forecasts ever.

**This is a weather instrument that was used in the past to measure snowfall.**

## Fact Box

The Greek word *meteoron* means "a thing in the sky." More than 2,300 years ago, a famous Greek scientist called Aristotle wrote a series of four books called *Meteorologica*. In these books, he made one of the first scientific attempts to explain the Earth's atmosphere and weather. The modern words *meteorology* and *meteorologist* were developed from Aristotle's books!

**1918–1921**
Cold and warm fronts are named by Vilhelm Bjerknes and a team of Norwegian meteorologists.

**1930s**
Radiosondes are first used in weather forecasting.

**1940s**
Radar is first used in weather forecasting.

**1950s**
Computers are first used in weather forecasting.

**1960**
*TIROS-I*, the first weather satellite, is launched.

**1980s**
Computer technology improves enormously, allowing better processing of weather information.

**1992–1996**
NEXRAD Next Generation Radar is installed in the United States, helping meteorologists give earlier, more accurate warnings of severe weather events such as storms and tornadoes.

# Important discoveries

Many important discoveries have helped meteorologists and other scientists learn more about the weather.

## Electricity in the sky

Storms often bring lightning and thunder, but until 1752 scientists did not know exactly what lightning was.

The American scientist Benjamin Franklin (1706–1790) suspected that lightning was a type of electricity, so he performed a dangerous experiment. He attached a wire to a kite and a key to the kite string. Then he flew the kite in a storm. Lightning was attracted to the metal on the kite and an electric spark was produced. He had proved that lightning was a type of electricity!

## Naming the clouds

For hundreds of years, meteorologists thought that naming clouds would be too difficult because their shapes change so easily. Then, in 1803, an English **amateur** meteorologist named Luke Howard (1772–1864) decided to use **Latin** words to name clouds.

He named four basic cloud types based on their appearance:

- *cumulus*, which is Latin for "heap"
- *nimbus*, which is Latin for "rain"
- *cirrus*, which is Latin for "hair"
- *stratus*, which is Latin for "layer"

Luke Howard's system of naming clouds has been expanded, but it is still used by meteorologists today.

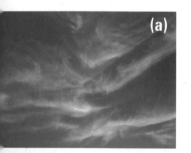

(a)

(b)

(c)

**These clouds are
(a) cirrus,
(b) cumulus, and
(c) a type of
stratus cloud.**

# Warm and cold fronts

Air masses are large areas of warm or cool air that form in the Earth's atmosphere over land, sea, and the frozen poles. Air masses move about the Earth's atmosphere, affecting our weather.

The boundaries or edges of air masses are called "fronts." A sudden change in temperature and wind direction often takes place when a front passes by. For example, when a "cold front" moves over a place where a warmer air mass has been, the temperature may drop several degrees in a few minutes! The wind may change direction and rain may fall.

Between 1918 and 1921, a team of meteorologists from Norway, led by Vilhelm Bjerknes, studied air masses. The team called the boundaries of air masses "fronts," naming them after the battle fronts in World War I. This was a very important discovery, because it helped meteorologists to understand more about changes in the weather and make better forecasts.

Bjerknes and his team also invented symbols for weather fronts that are still used on weather maps today.

**Weather maps use lines and symbols to describe air masses.**

# Weather on Mars

In 1976, two American spacecraft, the *Viking* landers, landed on Mars. The landers were spacecraft that worked as small weather stations, as well as collecting other scientific information. Meteorologists and other scientists learned much about Martian weather from the landers, and from other spacecraft that have since traveled to Mars. If astronauts travel to Mars in the future, accurate Martian weather forecasts will be needed.

**This is one of the *Viking* landers, which traveled to Mars in 1976.**

# El Niño and the Southern Oscillation

**To: Mark**
**From: Tony**
**Subject: El Niño**
**Attachment: Weather.doc**

Hi Mark

The winter weather here is very wet and stormy. There were big landslides around the San Francisco area, where I live, caused by the storms. Some roads and houses were damaged. We heard on the news that heavy rains are falling in other parts of the U.S. too, such as Florida. They are causing floods and crop damage. Dad says our troubles are caused by El Niño. I found a lot of information about it on the Internet. How is the weather in Australia?

Tony

**Weather.doc**

Every two to five years, a change of air pressure, winds, sea temperatures, and currents takes place over the Pacific Ocean. This is called the El Niño Southern Oscillation, or ENSO. Many people refer to ENSO simply as El Niño.

Normally, **trade winds** over the Pacific Ocean push warm seawater from east to west, towards Australia. This brings rain to Australia and some of its neighboring countries. A much colder ocean current flows up the west coast of South America. Fish depend on this cold current for food.

Every few years, weather patterns over the Pacific Ocean change. An area of low air pressure moves eastward and trade winds weaken, or reverse. This is called the Southern Oscillation. Warm water in the ocean then moves eastward and flows down the coast of South America. The warm current is called El Niño. El Niño causes warm, very wet winters in some parts of the U.S. and South America, and droughts in Australia.

## El Niño Southern Oscillation (ENSO)

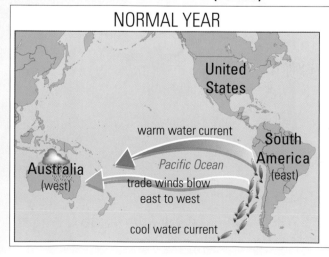

NORMAL YEAR

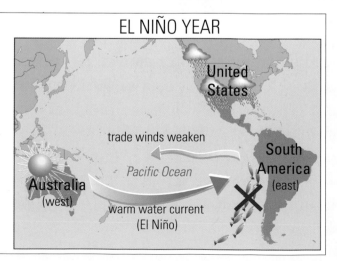

EL NIÑO YEAR

**To: Tony**
**From: Mark**
**Subject: El Niño**
**Attachment: ElNino.doc**

Hi Tony

The summer weather here is very hot and dry. Most of Australia is in the middle of a terrible drought. It has not rained for two months! We have very little water on our farm, and farmers cannot grow crops or feed their animals. El Niño is the cause of our troubles too.

Mark

El Niño.doc

More than 500 years ago, fishermen in Peru noticed a current of warm water in the ocean around Christmas time. Some years the current was warmer, and lasted longer. They called it El Niño, which means "boy child" in Spanish.

In 1923, a British scientist, Sir Gilbert Walker, discovered a connection between weather changes in countries on each side of the Pacific Ocean. In the 1960s, a Norwegian meteorologist working in the U.S., Jacob Bjerknes, made farther discoveries. He realized that changes in air pressure, weaker trade winds, and changing ocean currents combine to create ENSO events.

In 1982 and 1983, a very strong El Niño event caused storms, floods, and landslides in parts of the U.S. and South America. There were droughts in Australia and other western Pacific countries.

After this event, a network of weather **buoys** was set up in the Pacific Ocean to record changes in water temperature, winds, and air pressure. Information from the buoys allows scientists today to give several months' warning of a coming El Niño event. The system of weather buoys is maintained by the U.S. National Oceanic and Atmospheric Administration (NOAA), with the help of similar government organizations in Japan and France.

**This weather buoy detects ocean temperatures and weather conditions.**

# Training to be a meteorologist

Meteorologists work in a number of different fields, but they all need to learn certain common skills. Meteorologists become qualified by studying at college.

**Some meteorologists teach meteorology to others.**

## At school

Meteorology is a science, so high school students who want to become meteorologists need to study subjects such as physics, math, geography and English.

Subjects meteorologists use are:

- physics to help them understand the Earth's weather, climate, and atmosphere
- math to help them sort and study information about the weather
- geography to study weather all over the world
- English to communicate with other scientists, the media, and the public

## A college degree

After finishing high school, people who want to become meteorologists study a Bachelor of Science degree at college. While studying for their degree, they **major** in meteorology, and take many weather-related courses.

# Farther study

Meteorology students who have completed their bachelor's degree can do more study, called graduate study. Graduate students take advanced courses in meteorology, and do research in specific areas of meteorology. Graduate studies can take many years to complete.

After their final year of college, most students begin working as professional meteorologists.

# At work

Newly qualified meteorologists are ready to move into professional forecasting. Many begin working for government weather services in their country, such as the National Weather Service.

There are many other interesting positions available for meteorologists. Airports, the military, and aerospace agencies, such as the National Aeronautics and Space Administration (NASA), are just a few of the possible employers of weather forecasters.

# On-the-job training

Like most highly skilled scientists, meteorologists continue their education throughout their careers. They take courses to update their knowledge and learn the latest methods of weather forecasting.

Meteorologists are always learning!

**These meteorology students are getting practical experience.**

# Tools and instruments

Meteorologists use many different tools and instruments to gather information about the weather, climate, and atmosphere.

### Anemometers and anemomegraphs

Anemometers measure wind speed and direction. Anemomegraphs record changes in wind speed and direction over set periods of time.

**Anemometer**

### Barometers and barographs

Barometers measure air pressure. Air pressure changes as the atmosphere moves about. When air pressure is high, the weather is generally fine. When air pressure is low, it may rain. Barographs record changes in air pressure over set periods of time.

**Barometer**

### Hygrometers and hygrographs

Hygrometers measure humidity, which is the amount of water in the air. Some hygrometers contain a human hair. The hair changes in length, depending on the humidity of the air. Hygrographs record changes in humidity over set periods of time.

**Hygrometer**

### Thermometers and thermographs

Thermometers measure temperature. Different types of thermometers are used to record maximum and minimum temperatures, as well as ground or sea temperatures. Special wet-and-dry bulb thermometers are also used to record humidity. Thermographs record changes in temperature over set periods of time.

**Thermometers**

**Rain gauge**

## Rain gauges and pluviographs

Rain gauges measure rainfall. Pluviographs keep a record of rainfall over set periods of time.

**Radiosonde**

## Radiosondes and rawinsondes

Radiosondes are weather balloons that carry instruments and a radio transmitter high into the atmosphere. They gather information about weather conditions and send it back to meteorologists. Rawinsondes are weather balloons that are tracked by radar to measure wind speed and direction.

**Weather buoy**

## Weather buoys

Weather buoys at sea gather information on sea temperatures, wind speeds, and other weather conditions, far from land. Information is then transmitted back to weather offices.

**Satellite**

## Satellites

Satellites positioned over different parts of the Earth monitor weather conditions, sending pictures and information back to the Earth over set periods of time.

**Radar**

## Radar

Radar stands for **ra**dio **d**etection **a**nd **r**anging. It is a system of transmitting radio waves, which bounce back when they hit objects, showing the object's size, distance, and movement. Radar is used to track weather events such as rain, thunderstorms, and hurricanes.

**Computer**

## Computers

Computers are used to sort information received from weather observers and weather instruments. Satellite pictures, radar pictures, and weather maps are all created using computers. Computers are also used to create "models" of weather conditions and make predictions about future weather conditions.

# WEATHER EYES IN THE SKY

Today, seeing satellite pictures on daily weather forecasts is nothing special. We all take those pictures of Earth from far out in space for granted. But not so long ago there were no weather satellites. Without them, weather forecasting was much harder.

Satellites have many uses. They can be used for scientific research, communications, or even spying on other countries. The first satellite was launched on October 4, 1957 by Russian scientists. It was called *Sputnik 1* and it orbited Earth for 57 days. Soon many satellites were launched by other countries. Scientists realized how useful weather satellites could be. Satellites could give advance warnings of dangerous weather events, and help meteorologists make more accurate weather forecasts.

The first weather satellite, *TIROS-1*, was launched in the U.S. on April 1, 1960. It carried two special television cameras, and it sent back the first-ever pictures of cloud patterns and storms from space.

*TIROS-1* was a huge success. It operated for 78 days and sent thousands of pictures back to Earth.

## Fact Box

*TIROS-1* was a **polar orbiting satellite**. Polar orbiting satellites circle Earth at heights of around 518 miles (833 km). Other satellites hover in one place above the Earth, much farther out in space. At heights of around 22,245 miles (35,800 km), they take pictures over much larger areas.

This *TIROS* satellite is attached to a rocket for launching.

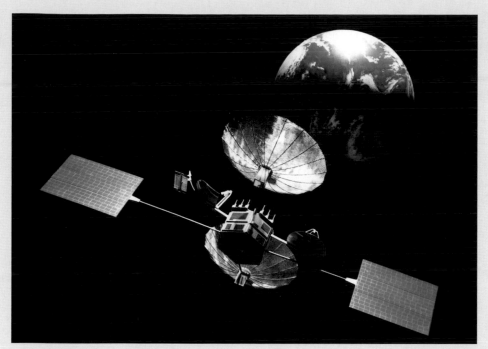

**This is a modern satellite.**

After the success of *TIROS-1*, more weather satellites were launched. As weather satellites and instruments improved, satellite pictures were sent to weather offices around the world. This helped meteorologists in every country to make better weather forecasts.

Today, weather satellites from several countries provide information on weather conditions on every part of the Earth, both on land and at sea. They monitor temperatures on land, at sea, and at different levels in the atmosphere. They also provide information on cloud patterns, storms, hurricanes, wind speeds, sea ice, and many other weather-related matters.

Weather satellites also collect information sent by other weather instruments, such as weather buoys in the oceans and weather balloons in the air. This important information is then transmitted back to weather offices.

Since 1960, weather satellites have been providing information that saves lives. They have given advance warnings of dangerous weather conditions, so people could prepare for them. For more than 40 years, those amazing weather eyes in the sky have been watching over us, helping meteorologists make better weather forecasts!

# Modern methods

Meteorologists work in the field and at weather bureaus. They use the latest technology to help them study weather conditions and the atmosphere.

## In the field

On land, information on weather conditions is collected at weather stations, using a range of modern instruments.

In the air, weather information is collected by aircraft. Passenger aircraft gather information on weather conditions. Weather balloons are released to gather information about conditions high in the atmosphere. Satellites monitor weather conditions from high above the Earth.

At sea, ships can monitor weather conditions. Weather buoys at sea also collect information on sea temperatures and weather conditions.

## At the weather bureau

The information gathered is sent to weather bureaus and offices by e-mail, fax, and satellite. This allows meteorologists to receive weather information quickly. They can then use it to predict upcoming weather, together with information collected using instruments such as radar.

weather station collects data

data is sent by satellite

## Using computers

When weather information is gathered at weather bureaus or offices, it is entered into huge computers. These "supercomputers" are extremely powerful and can process enormous amounts of information at great speed. Computer programs that model the weather based on weather information are also used by meteorologists. They help predict upcoming weather, or climate changes caused by events such as El Niño.

**A weather map contains many different symbols.**

Weather charts showing air pressure, wind patterns, and other weather conditions are usually produced by computers, although they are sometimes hand-drawn by meteorologists.

## Producing weather forecasts

Computers and computer programs are very important tools, but they cannot replace a meteorologist! Meteorologists study the information that has been processed by computers. They study charts showing current weather conditions, observe changes in weather conditions hour by hour, and then use their expert knowledge to produce weather forecasts.

## Broadcasting the forecast

Once weather forecasts have been produced, they must be broadcast to those who need to know the weather. Modern methods of broadcasting the weather mean that everyone can get up-to-date forecasts at any time. Weather forecasts appear on the Internet, television, radio, and in newspapers.

data is used to prepare weather forecast

weather forecast is broadcast to public

# Working on location

Weather conditions around the world are very different. Studying different types of weather conditions on location can present many exciting challenges for meteorologists.

## Antarctic weather

There are 40 permanent bases in Antarctica, belonging to several different countries. Meteorologists and many other scientists live and work at the bases for weeks or months at a time to study Antarctic weather.

Weather forecasters in Antarctica have a difficult job, because Antarctic weather is very unpredictable. Weather information is gathered from **automatic weather stations** set up in different parts of Antarctica. It is also gathered from satellites, weather balloons, and from observations made by meteorologists and other weather observers at each base. Then meteorologists in weather offices at the larger bases make weather forecasts.

Accurate weather forecasts are very important in Antarctica because the weather conditions can be very dangerous for ships, aircraft, and land vehicles. In Antarctica, lives depend on good weather forecasting.

**A weather forecaster working in Antarctica**

# Tornadoes

Some meteorologists work in the field, studying tornadoes and trying to learn more about them. They follow reports of tornadoes and "chase" them. They leave instruments in the path of tornadoes, to measure the temperature, air pressure, and humidity inside them. They film tornadoes to watch the way they behave.

Tornadoes can destroy homes and property.

Tornadoes are very violent thunderstorms, with huge spinning columns of wind that reach down from the clouds and touch the ground. Tornadoes can form when cold and warm air masses meet and the atmosphere is very stormy.

Tornadoes are very destructive. Winds inside them can reach more than 280 miles (450 km) per hour! They move along the ground, tearing up and destroying everything in their path. Many people have been killed by tornadoes.

Tornadoes form in most countries of the world. They are very common in some parts of the U.S. during spring. Meteorologists at the United States National Weather Service broadcast tornado warnings to help protect lives and property. They use a special type of radar, called Doppler radar, to track the movement of winds, to see if it is likely that tornadoes may form. They are able to tell if a tornado will form around 30 to 60 minutes before it does.

Meteorologists are learning more about tornadoes so that they can predict them earlier and help save more lives and property.

## Fact Box

People other than meteorologists enjoy chasing tornadoes as a hobby. Some adventure companies even take tourists tornado-chasing!

# Donna Dubberke, meteorologist

Donna Dubberke is a warning coordination meteorologist in a forecast office with the National Weather Service.

### What does your job involve?

About 20 percent of my time is spent working as a forecaster. The rest of the time I work with the media and the community, educating them and helping them prepare for hazardous weather.

### When did you first become interested in meteorology?

For as long as I can remember, I was always interested in the outdoors and the sky. On vacations, I used to make my parents stop the car so I could take pictures of the clouds! In about the seventh grade, I decided I wanted to become a meteorologist.

### Where did you study and what qualifications did you obtain?

I took all of the math and science I could in high school, then went to college at the University of Oklahoma. I earned bachelor's degrees in meteorology and math.

### What was your first job as a meteorologist? Where have you worked since then?

While I was a student in college, I worked part-time at the National Severe Storms Laboratory in Norman, Oklahoma. Since I graduated, I have worked in the National Weather Service at different field forecast offices. I was a meteorological intern in Fort Worth, Texas, then a general forecaster in Norman, Oklahoma, for five years. I moved to Davenport, Iowa, as a senior forecaster in the late 1990s, then just last year became warning coordination meteorologist for our office.

**What do you like most about your job?**

I like making a difference. Whether we are teaching people about weather safety, helping a community develop their preparedness strategy, issuing a forecast that helps people plan, or issuing a warning that prompts someone to take action and protect themselves, we impact on people's lives. It feels good to know that I've helped people in some way.

**What do you like least about your job?**

The paperwork. Every job requires a certain amount of tracking and paperwork, and this job is no exception! I really don't like that part.

**What are the difficulties and dangers of your job?**

One of the most difficult things I've ever done was in June of 2001. A tornado was heading right for the small town where I live, and I was at work. We issued the tornado warning and I had to wait until after it passed to find out if my family was okay. There aren't many direct dangers with this job. No matter what the weather is, we still have to be at work. So sometimes that does mean driving to work in heavy snow, dense fog, or hailstones.

**What was your most exciting meteorological project?**

I worked during the Mississippi River floods of 2001 in Davenport. I was also on duty when a large tornado tracked through an amusement park in Oklahoma City, in June of 1988. In college I helped with a storm electricity project where we used high-speed cameras to photograph intra-cloud lightning from thunderstorms that were overhead. That was neat.

**What advice would you give to young people interested in a career in meteorology?**

Take as many science and math classes as you can and learn about computers. When it comes time to get a job, find a way to stand out from the crowd, such as getting experience to go with your schooling.

**Meteorologists monitoring a hurricane**

# Hurricane Camille

Hurricane Camille was one of the worst hurricanes ever to hit the U.S. Read the hurricane diary to find out more.

## Fact Box

Meteorologists issue a hurricane watch for an area where a hurricane may arrive within 36 hours. They issue a hurricane warning for an area where a hurricane is going to arrive within 24 hours or less.

**A beach in Biloxi, Mississippi, after Hurricane Camille passed**

### Thursday August 14, 1969

In the warm seas south of Cuba, a tropical storm is identified. A U.S. Navy airplane pilot finds low air pressure at its center; a warning sign that a hurricane is forming. Meteorologists name the storm Camille.

### Friday August 15, 1969

Camille's strong winds form a circular pattern as she moves north. She has become a hurricane! Meteorologists track her on radar as she passes western Cuba. Powerful winds churn up the sea and create huge waves. Rain pours down on Cuba. In the U.S., meteorologists warn of the hurricane's strength.

### Saturday August 16, 1969

By Saturday morning, Camille is closer to the U.S. Meteorologists monitor her by radar and satellite. They issue a hurricane watch for areas of the Florida and Mississippi coast. Within hours, they issue hurricane warnings. Another Navy airplane flies into the storm, measuring wind speeds of around 150 miles (240 km) per hour.

### Sunday August 17, 1969

Hurricane warnings continue as Camille moves farther north. People living by the sea are **evacuated**. A final flight finds winds of around 200 miles (320 km) per hour close to Camille's center. Finally, late on Sunday night, she hits the Mississippi coast. Huge winds tear at buildings, the sea is pushed inland, and floods destroy whole towns.

### Monday August 18, 1969

By Monday, the worst of Hurricane Camille has passed. She begins to weaken as she moves inland and travels north through Mississippi. By the time she reaches the border of Mississippi and Tennessee, she is no longer a hurricane, but an area of rain.

**Wreckage left by Hurricane Camille in Mississippi in August 1969**

### Tuesday August 19, 1969

When the remains of Hurricane Camille reach the states of Virginia and West Virginia, the rains become much heavier. On Tuesday night, they cause terrible floods and landslides. Many people lose their lives.

### Wednesday August 20–Friday August 22, 1969

The remains of Camille finally move away from the U.S. and back out to sea. On August 22, she is absorbed into a cold front, south of Newfoundland.

More than 200 people died during the hurricane, and in the floods and landslides that followed.

**Fact Box**

Hurricanes are rated on a special scale, called the Saffir-Simpson Scale.

Category 1 hurricanes cause minimal damage.

Category 5 hurricanes cause catastrophic damage.

Hurricane Camille was a Category 5 hurricane.

# Meteorology in the future

The science of meteorology has changed a lot in the past 100 years. What will meteorology be like in the future?

## Climate change and meteorology

Over millions of years, the Earth's climate has changed many times. During ice ages, the weather was much cooler. At other times in the Earth's history, the Earth was much warmer. The Earth's climate is still slowly changing, but some of this change may now be due to human activity.

The Earth is like a giant greenhouse. Gases in the atmosphere trap heat from the sun, reflecting it back to Earth. This is called the greenhouse effect and it helps keep the planet warm.

The Earth's climate is presently becoming warmer. This is called global warming. The burning of **fossil fuels** such as coal and oil is increasing the amount of **greenhouse gases** in the Earth's atmosphere. Some scientists believe the increase in greenhouse gases may be increasing global warming.

In the future, global warming may cause the weather and climate to change or become more unpredictable in some places on Earth. There may be more rain and storms in some parts of the world, and less in others. Weather forecasting will become more challenging with climate change.

**The Earth's atmosphere traps some of the Sun's heat.**

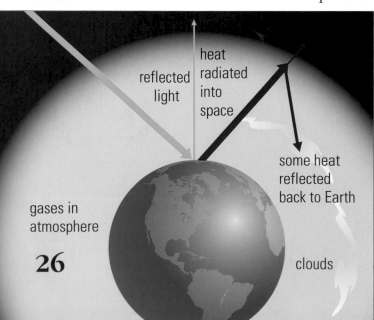

reflected light

heat radiated into space

some heat reflected back to Earth

gases in atmosphere

clouds

# Future weather forecasts

It will probably never be possible to stop thunderstorms from forming or to prevent hurricanes from causing damage. However, accurate warnings of these and other severe weather conditions help save lives and property around the world every day.

In the future, a range of newer and even better weather instruments than those available today will be invented. Computers will become more powerful and computer programs that predict upcoming weather conditions will become more accurate.

With the help of new weather instruments and information, meteorologists will be able to provide even more accurate weather forecasts, even farther into the future. A closer "weather eye" will be kept on the planet, helping the public to plan their week, farmers to plan the best time for planting crops, emergency services to prepare for severe weather, and air and sea transportation, to travel safely around the world.

More will be learned about weather events such as El Niño and global warming, too.

The future of weather forecasting is looking bright!

**This is next-generation radar – a U.S. NEXRAD installation.**

# Get involved in meteorology

You can get involved in meteorology by studying the weather at home or at school. Here are some fun activities that you might like to try.

## Make a rain gauge

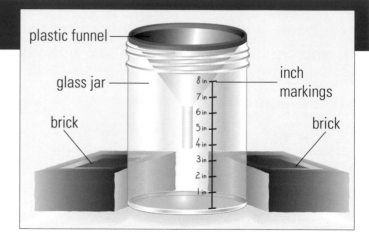

plastic funnel

glass jar

brick

8 in
7 in
6 in
5 in
4 in
3 in
2 in
1 in

inch markings

brick

**You will need:**

- wide-mouthed jar with straight sides
- marker pen and ruler
- small plastic funnel that will fit firmly into the top of the jar
- scotch tape
- two bricks or rocks
- notebook

**What to do:**

1 Rain is measured in inches or millimeters. Use the pen and ruler to mark the side of the jar.

2 Place the plastic funnel inside the top of the jar and tape it in place. The funnel should fit nicely on the top of the jar.

3 Stand the rain gauge in an open place, away from trees, fences, or other objects. Stand it between two bricks or rocks, so it doesn't blow over in windy weather.

4 Check the amount of rain collected in the rain gauge each day and record it in your notebook. Don't forget to empty the rain gauge each day after you have recorded the amount.

## Measure the air temperature

Meteorologists use several types of thermometers to measure air temperature. Hang a thermometer outside in a place where the sun will not shine directly on it, and record the air temperature in your notebook each day.

# Make a barometer

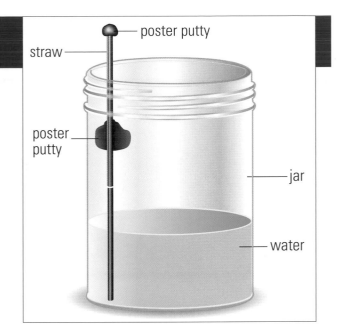

straw — poster putty
poster putty
jar
water

**You will need:**

- clean glass jar
- straw
- marker pen
- poster putty
- water
- notebook

**What to do:**

**1** Fill the jar one-third full with water. Place the straw in the water and attach it to the side of the jar with some poster putty. Don't let the straw touch the bottom of the jar.

**2** Suck the water halfway up the straw. At the same time, pinch the top of the straw to keep the water in the tube. Quickly stick some poster putty over the top of the straw, so the water stays in the tube. Make a mark on the straw at the water level.

**3** Keep your barometer inside. Check the water level in the straw each day. It will rise when air pressure is high and air is pressing down on the water in the glass, forcing it up the straw. This happens when fine weather is likely. The water will fall when air pressure is low. Then it may rain.

**4** Record your observations in your notebook each day.

# Watch the sky

Observing clouds will help you to forecast the weather. You can buy cloud charts from your nearest weather office or download them from the Internet. Use a cloud chart to identify cloud types and record what weather you see.

# More to do

Get your whole class involved in meteorology!

- Set up a school weather station.
- Publish a weekly weather report in your school newsletter.
- Ask a meteorologist to give a talk to your class.

# Check it out!

Meteorology is an exciting science. You can learn more about meteorology, and the job of meteorologists, by checking out some of these places and Web sites.

## Weather offices

Most cities and states have a local weather office or weather bureau. Many weather offices run guided tours. You can learn more about the science of meteorology by visiting a weather office near you. Most national weather offices have Web sites.

**United States National Oceanic and Atmospheric Administration (NOAA)**   http://www.noaa.gov

**United States National Weather Service**
http://www.nws.noaa.gov

**National Weather Service Tropical Prediction Center – National Hurricane Center**   http://www.nhc.noaa.gov

## Weather clubs and associations

There are many clubs and associations in the U.S. and around the world for those who are interested in the weather. Some clubs are for those who are interested in storm chasing, tornadoes, and other severe weather events. Others are for people who are interested in the weather in general.

## Web sites

**National Weather Association**   http://www.nwas.org
**World Meteorological Association**   http://www.wmo.ch/index-en.html

# Glossary

**air pressure**   the pressure or force of the Earth's atmosphere in any given place

**amateur**   someone who does something for pleasure, rather than doing it as a paid job

**atmosphere**   the gases that surround a planet

**atmospheric sciences**   sciences that involve the study of the Earth's atmosphere, such as meteorology and climatology

**automatic weather stations**   weather stations that are not occupied by people, but automatically transmit information on weather conditions to weather offices

**buoys**   special types of floats, often anchored out at sea

**climate**   the general weather conditions of a particular place, for example the cold climate of Antarctica

**evacuated**   taken away or removed from an area

**folklore**   traditional beliefs, stories, and legends of different peoples

**fossil fuels**   fuels such as coal, oil, or gas, formed from the remains of plants and animals that lived millions of years ago

**greenhouse gases**   gases in the Earth's atmosphere that stop some of the sun's heat from escaping from the Earth

**hurricanes**   large tropical storms with very strong winds that blow in a circular pattern (known as tropical cyclones in the Australian region and typhoons in Southeast Asia)

**Latin**   a very old type of language first spoken in ancient Rome. Many Latin words are still used today

**Norse mythology**   traditional stories of fiction from Norway, usually about imaginary people or creatures

**polar orbiting satellite**   a satellite that orbits the Earth from north to south, crossing above the north and south poles

**radar**   a system of sending radio waves, used to track weather events such as rain, thunderstorms, and hurricanes

**superstition**   ideas and beliefs that are not based on scientific fact or reason, and are often incorrect

**telegraph**   a communications system invented in the early 1800s. In early telegraph systems, pulses of electricity were sent along an electrical cable at different rates, forming a code that could be read at the other end.

**tornadoes**   very violent thunderstorms, with enormous spinning columns of wind that reach down from the clouds and touch the ground

**trade winds**   winds that blow over the ocean in a westerly direction (from southeast to northwest in the southern hemisphere and from northeast to southwest in the northern hemisphere)

# Index